T0191189

PRICELESS
FACTS
ABOUT
MONEY

First edition 2024

Library of Congress Catalog Card Number 2024934315
ISBN 978-1-5362-2471-9

24 25 26 27 28 29 CCP 10 9 8 7 6 5 4 3 2

Printed in Shenzhen, Guangdong, China

This book was typeset in ITC Stone Informal.
The illustrations were done in ink and watercolor wash and completed digitally.

Candlewick Press
99 Dover Street
Somerville, Massachusetts 02144

www.candlewick.com

PRICELESS
FACTS
ABOUT
MONEY

MELLODY HOBSON
with NELL SCOVELL

ILLUSTRATED BY
CAITLIN STEVENS

CANDLEWICK PRESS

For Everest and children everywhere
MH

For my mother
CS

CONTENTS

John: Hi, Mellody. Want to play?
Mellody: Not right now, John. I'm writing a book.

John: About what?
Mellody: Money.

John: Oh, I already know a lot about money.

Mellody: Did you know that the ancient Maya civilization used chocolate as an early form of cash?

John: No, but I wish we still did that. What else is in there?

Mellody: Lots of weird and fun facts, like cinnamon and sugar helped create the stock market . . . medieval knights carried unusual credit cards . . . and a $100 bill contains hidden messages.

John: Exciting! Could I help you?

Mellody: Of course! Let's start by introducing ourselves.

MEET MELLODY AND JOHN

My name is Mellody. I grew up in Chicago as the youngest of six kids raised by a single mom. When I was little, I loved school and dreamed of being a grown-up. My favorite games were playing store and office. I even kept all my favorite things in a real briefcase that I carried with me.

School wasn't the only place where I learned stuff. My mom wanted to make sure I knew how much things cost, so she would always give me money to pay at a store or restaurant. When I got older, I learned to count the change. As I got better at math, I was able to figure out tips and double-check the bill.

Like most kids, I knew the price of candy, but I also knew that a steak cost more than a hamburger. My mom used to show me the phone bill, the electricity bill, and the water bill. (Yep, tap water costs money.) She even told me how much we paid each month to live in our apartment. These added up to the "cost of living."

Even though my mom worked really, really hard, she couldn't always afford to pay our bills. Sometimes our phone or electricity would be cut off. We also had to move a lot. Those scary times made me want to understand how money worked.

As I got older, I started reading and asking questions. And the more I learned, the more I thought . . . money is *mesmerizing*! One summer during college, I got a job working for a man named John who knew *a lot* about money. Amazingly, more than thirty years later, I still work with John. Together, we run a company that helps people invest their money so their savings will grow, and they can pay for the life they want.

No matter how much or how little you have, everyone has to deal with money. Understanding it can help you master it. Today, I get to work in a real office. I love my grown-up job, and each day I learn more about how money works.

Money is not a thing. Still, the remains of plants and dinosaurs from this time period will eventually turn into the coal, oil, and gas that run factories, heat homes, and power non-electric cars. That's why they're called fossil fuels.

130,000 Years Ago
HUMANS, NO DINOSAURS

Ancient humans known as Neanderthals (*nee-AN-der-tahls*) roam around Europe and Asia. Money is still not a thing.

50,000 Years Ago
HUNTING AND GATHERING

Modern humans evolved in Africa more than 315,000 years ago. They are named *Homo sapiens* (*hoh-moh SAY-pee-ens*), which is Latin for "wise man." They learn to talk and trade, and probably argue. But not about money, because physical money is still not a thing.

Hi. My name is John. I grew up in Chicago as an only child. My mother was the first Black woman to graduate from the University of Chicago Law School. My father was one of the famous Tuskegee (pronounced *tuh-SKEE-gee*) Airmen who flew airplanes during World War II. My dad grew up in the 1930s, during a hard time known as the Great Depression when a lot of businesses closed, people couldn't find jobs, and many went hungry. I was born several decades later, but those tough years made a big impression on my father. He wanted to make sure that I knew about money and how to make it last and grow.

On Christmas morning, a lot of kids find presents under the tree. Instead, I found a white envelope. Inside that envelope was a stock certificate (an official piece of paper). That was my dad's gift to me. He explained that this certificate meant I owned a tiny part—or share— of that company. My dad also explained that if the company made money, I might even receive a cash "dividend" (*DIH-vuh-dend*) as an owner. If I wanted to buy a candy bar with that money, I could. I was a twelve-year-old with cash in my pocket. Yeah!

By the way, I liked basketball a lot, too. I played for my college team, but I wasn't quite good enough to turn pro. I continued to invest in companies like my dad taught me, and that hobby became my passion. Today, I run an investment company with my business partner and friend, Mellody. The two of us talk about money all the time, and it's never boring.

MONEY BECOMES A THING!

Farming grows into a big business in Mesopotamia (*meh-so-po-TAY-mee-ah*), the area between two rivers in the Middle East. People settle and a civilization thrives. In order to buy goods (like food and wood) and services (like construction work and haircuts), people need a way to trade. They create a system of coins with an agreed-upon value. The first currency (*KER-en-see*) is called "shekels" (*SHEH-kuls*). Shekels are coins that weigh a set amount. In fact, "shekel" comes from the Hebrew word meaning "to weigh." Money is finally a thing!

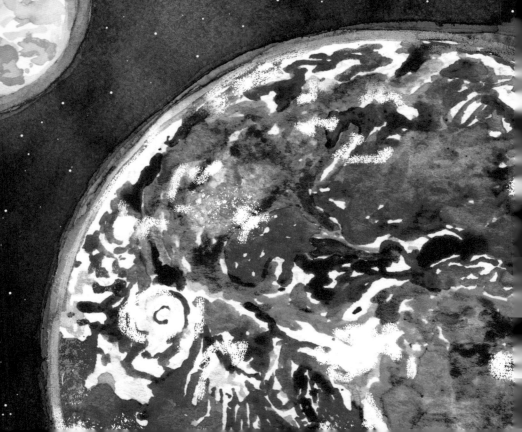

A Short
History of Money

(All dates are approximate.)

3.9 Billion Years Ago
THE FIRST BANK DEPOSIT

A very, very, very(!) long time ago, meteorites crashed into our planet, scattering valuable metals like gold and platinum all across the earth.

John: Hey, Mellody. Is that a cupcake?
Mellody: Yes, John. I made it myself.

John: It looks so good.
Mellody: That's because I baked it with love. And chocolate.

John: Would you be willing to trade the cupcake for something?

Mellody: Yes! I love bartering!

John: What's bartering?
Mellody: That's the word for when people trade stuff of similar value. Before cash was a thing, it was how people made deals.

John: I see. So what would I have to trade you for a cupcake?
Mellody: How about you give me your basketball?
John: No way! My basketball is worth more than a cupcake.

Mellody: What else do you have?
John: A piece of yarn.
Mellody: What's it for?

10,000 Years Ago
FARMING BEGINS

Humans learn how to grow plants and raise animals, which means they no longer need to roam around in search of their next meal. Farming allows them to stay in one place for a long time. Villages form. Money is still not a thing.

John: To remind me to keep my wrist straight when I'm shooting baskets.

Mellody: I don't need that. Also, I already have a piece of yarn.

John: Then how about a basketball lesson? Or a bag of potato chips?

Mellody: Neither of those has the same value to me as this cupcake.

John: I know! What about this drawing I made? It's the airplane that my dad flew in World War II. It took me a long time to get the wings right.

Mellody: I love art! And that drawing is definitely worth a cupcake.

John: Wait. I just realized that if I eat this cupcake, I'll have nothing, and you'll still have the drawing.

Mellody: But you'll have the experience of eating the cupcake. That experience has value.

John: I'd like to experience that chocolate icing. Let's trade.

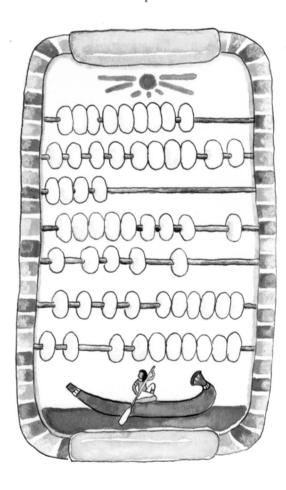

Ancient Egyptian traders who worked along the Nile River used a counting machine called an "abacus" (A-buh-kuhs) to add large numbers quickly. Amazingly, the abacus is still in use today.

Flipping a coin is a way to use chance to make a decision. During the Roman Empire, some coins had a ship on one side and the head of the emperor on the other, so early coin-flippers were asked to choose between "ship or head?" Later that became "Heads or tails?"

2,000 Years Ago COINS TELL STORIES	1,500 Years Ago CHOCOLATE IS PRECIOUS

Thanks to coins, we know a lot about history. For example, we know the exact year that the Colosseum stadium opened because the ancient Romans stamped a coin to mark the occasion. Coins also tell us that the kingdom of Aksum in eastern Africa (where Ethiopia and Eritrea are today) was a trading empire with a ruler named Nezool. This civilization prospered for centuries, and coins from Aksum have been found as far away as India.

In Central America, ancient Maya accepted cacao (*kuh-KOW*) beans as payment for taxes since everyone agreed they were worth a lot. And why were the beans so valuable? Because they could be roasted, crushed, mixed with spices, and combined with hot water to make hot chocolate. Yum!

Paper money was first created in China using bark from mulberry trees. Later, guards had to stand watch over the mulberry forests so thieves could not sneak in and strip off bark to make their own money.

BARK!

CHHHARRGGGEEE IT!

In the Middle Ages, some knights wore special rings that could be pressed into hot wax to leave a unique mark. That signet ring was their signature! So if a knight needed a new set of armor, he might give the blacksmith a written promise to pay and seal the note with his ring. That note could later be exchanged for cash at the castle that hired the knight.

GOODS FOR SALE

John: What's wrong, Mellody?

Mellody: I wanted to buy a book, but the bookstore wouldn't let me pay with a cupcake.

John: Bartering doesn't always work. That's why we have money.

Mellody: So I can't trade cupcakes for books, but I can sell my cupcakes and then use that money to buy a book?

John: Exactly! That's how currency works.

Mellody: Fascinating.
One more question.

John: Yes?

Mellody: Would you like to buy a cupcake?

John: Sorry, but I already had that experience.

In 1602, the Dutch East India Company started trading coffee, fabrics, and spices like cinnamon and sugar all over the world. This business was very successful. Years later, the company wanted to grow. They needed to build more ships, which required money. That's when someone came up with a new idea: they could raise funds by selling small pieces of the company. These pieces became known as "stocks" or "shares," and the people who bought them were called "investors." If the company made more money over time, the shares went up in value and the investors could sell them at a profit. If the shares went down in value, the investors would lose money. This fresh idea spread worldwide. Today, lots of corporations trade shares (or stocks) on what is called a "stock exchange," which connects buyers with sellers. The biggest stock exchanges today are located in New York, London, Tokyo, Shanghai, Mumbai, and Hong Kong.

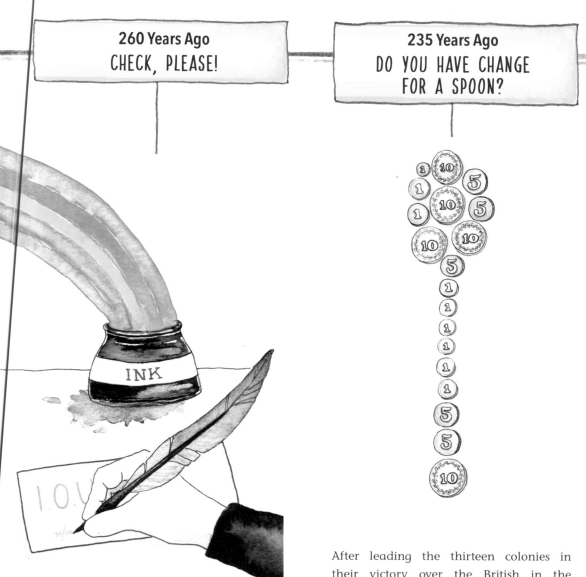

After leading the thirteen colonies in their victory over the British in the American Revolution, General George Washington was elected as the first president of the United States. A new country needs money, so legend has it that Washington asked his wife for a favor. Martha Washington—the very first First Lady—came from a wealthy family and agreed to donate her silver spoons, knives, and forks to be melted down into coins for the new nation.

The IOU—shortened from the phrase "I owe you" and coined in the 1600s—is a written note that keeps track of a debt. In 1762, a British banker had the idea to print these IOUs and include special numbers so bankers could "check" on the amount. This may be how paper checks got their name.

19

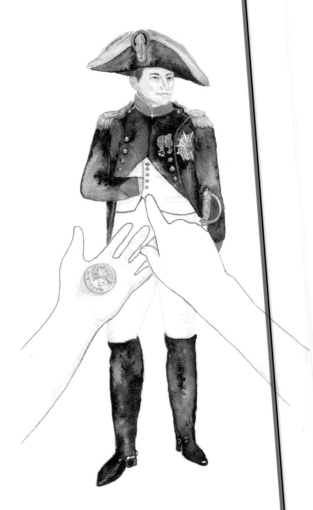

Alexander Hamilton served as the first secretary of the Treasury, a.k.a. the country's top banker. The United States spent a lot of money fighting the British to gain independence, and to pay off those debts, Hamilton created a way for people to invest in the future of the young nation. He sold those investments—called "bonds"—from his home at 58 Wall Street in New York. Centuries later, Wall Street remains home to scores of financial companies.

After the French Revolution, Napoleon Bonaparte crowned himself emperor of France in 1804. He quickly ordered new money stamped with his face. Why? Because coins were an easy way for people across Europe to know what their new conqueror looked like.

At the end of a nice dinner at a New York City restaurant, a businessman couldn't find his wallet and was unable to pay for his meal. Embarrassed, he went home and invented a system that allowed diners to pay their bill with a card instead of cash. He called it the "Diners Club card," and it was the first charge card. Initially made out of paper, credit cards are now plastic or metal and commonly used everywhere.

Thanks to technology, people can now pay for items and services without cash by linking their smartphones to their bank accounts. This is called a digital debit (*DEH-bit*) card, and purchases can be made with the wave of a phone.

For a long time, bank tellers were human beings. They stood behind counters and took care of customers, turning checks into cash and depositing money into accounts. Then technology created machines that could do these same tasks. Plus, the machines never had to sleep and could stay open all night. The first ATM (automated teller machine) popped up in London in 1967. Today, ATMs are all over the world. Still, most banks have some human tellers because machines can't do everything.

HIDDEN TREASURE

Mellody: John! Want to help me build a sandcastle?

John: No can do, Mell. I'm searching for buried treasure with this metal detector.

Mellody: What sort of things might be hiding in the sand?

John: Gold coins from pirate ships . . . diamond rings . . . a key to another dimension . . .

Mellody: And what have you found?

John: Seven bottle caps. Two buttons. A toy car and a spoon.

Mellody: Hey, it's beeping.

John: Yes! A nickel. I knew this would pay off!

Mellody: How long have you been searching for stuff on the beach?

John: Two hours.

Mellody: And you made five cents. Do the math, John. That means you've earned two and a half cents per hour.

John: I guess searching for buried treasure isn't the best way to get rich.

Mellody: No. But it's a nice way to spend a day at the beach. And if it helps, you could pretend that these bottle caps are pirate booty. Ha! That word always makes me laugh.

John: Arrrrgh.

Mellody: Hey, you sound just like a pirate!

John: No. Arrrrgh, I just found another bottle cap with my foot detector.

NICKNAMES FOR MONEY

Do you have a nickname? Maybe even more than one? Over the years, money has been given a lot of nicknames. Here are some of the most famous ones.

Bacon

There are many theories for how "bacon" became a nickname for money. Some believe the phrase comes from the 1500s when county fairs held contests to see which villager could catch a greased pig. The prize for catching the slippery pig was . . . the pig. So the winner actually got to "bring home the bacon."

Bread and Dough

Bread is one of the most common foods, and each region has its own special type. There's the French baguette, Indian naan, Chinese mantou, and more. Because it's so important, "bread" has become another nickname for money along with "dough," which when baked becomes . . . bread.

Bucks

A buck is a male deer, and in the 1700s, deerskins were sometimes used for trading.

Cha-ching!

This nickname refers to the sound that a cash register used to make when completing a sale. It's often used to celebrate. For example: "I just made $10 selling lemonade. Cha-ching!"

Cheddar

At the end of World War II, the United States suffered from food shortages, so the government sent packages to the needy. These care packages sometimes included a chunk of cheddar. The cheese was so valued that it became a nickname for money.

Clams

In the 1600s, Native Americans in the Northeast traded with wampumpeag (*WAHM-pum-peeg*), which was a currency made from polished shells like clams. Wampumpeag was one of the first widely accepted currencies of early America.

C-notes

"C" is the Roman numeral for 100 (from the Latin word *centum*), so a $100 bill is called a "C-note."

Dead Presidents

Bills are also known as "dead presidents," although this is not factually true. Alexander Hamilton and Benjamin Franklin are both pictured on US bills and never even had that job.

A Grand

"Grand" is another word for "large," and in the early 1900s, a thousand dollars was a large amount of money—one might even say a "grand" amount.

Greenbacks

This early nickname for money came from the green ink used on the back of US bills. The color green was chosen because photography at the time was only in black-and-white, and using green ink meant no one could take a picture of a bill and pass it off as real money.

Lettuce/Cabbage/Spinach

You might think that these three vegetables became nicknames for money because they're also green, but etymologists (*eh-tuh-MAH-luh-jists*)—people who study where words come from—cannot prove that theory. It's a mystery. (Only the spinach knows the truth, and it's not talking.)

Moola

Another mystery involves referring to money as "moola." Some say the nickname started in France. Others say Ireland. Still others say the Fiji Islands. So where in the world did the word "moola" come from?

Smackeroonies

"Smackers" referred to the sound a stack of cash makes when it's smacked into the palm of a hand. Later, "smackers" turned into "smackeroonies," which is longer but more fun to say.

ALLOWANCE

John: You got a book! Did you sell all your cupcakes?

Mellody: Yes, but I didn't earn quite enough, so I had to add in some money I received for my birthday.

John: I would have used the allowance I get for doing chores at home like folding laundry and taking out the trash.

Mellody: My mom says chores are part of living in our house, so I don't get paid for them.

John: Really? I guess different families have different feelings and ideas about money.

Mellody: They sure do. So how do you spend your allowance?

John: Sometimes I use it to buy something I want right now. Sometimes I donate my allowance to charities or others in need. Sometimes I save for months until I have enough to buy something more expensive like a Chicago Bulls jersey.

Mellody: My grandma likes to give money as gifts, and one year I saved my Christmas gift, my birthday gift, and my tooth fairy money so I had enough to adopt a koala bear.

John: Really? I've never seen you walking a koala.

Mellody: That's because my koala lives in Australia. Her name is Creaky, which is also the sound she makes.

John: Do you think you'll ever get to visit Creaky in Australia?

Mellody: Yes, but I'll have to save for a long time to do that.

MY WALLET HOLDS A MYSTERY

Mellody: I love my wallet.

John: Can I see what's inside?

Mellody: Sure. In this pouch, I have some coins.

John: What's that big one?

Mellody: It's a dollar with Susan B. Anthony on it. She demanded voting rights for women.

John: Susie B!

Mellody: Yep. She was the first woman on a US coin.

John: Who was the second?

Mellody: The Native American explorer Sacagawea (*Sa-kuh-juh-WEE-uh*). She was a member of the Shoshone (*shuh-SHOW-nee*) tribe and, as a teenager, helped make a map of the West.

John: What else do you keep in your wallet?

Mellody: My student ID. And this special piece of yarn.

John: What makes that yarn so special?

Mellody: It's kind of personal. I should put it back in my wallet. I don't want to lose it.

Student Name:
Mellody Hobson

Identification Number:
04041988143

AROUND THE GLOBE

Not only do different countries have different languages, but they also have different types of money. In 2020, the United Nations recognized 180 currencies across the globe. This means that when you travel, your bills from home probably won't be accepted in the land you're visiting. Fortunately, in the same way that we can translate languages, we can exchange money from one country into money from another.

EXCUSE ME

John: Sorry for the interruption, but I wanted to mention that when my family went to England for a vacation, our dollars weren't accepted. We had to use pounds.

Mellody: What are pounds?

John: They're what English people use instead of dollars.

Mellody: I thought a pound was a unit of weight?

John: Yes, but in England they weigh things in stones.

Mellody: So dollars are pounds and pounds are stones? This is so confusing.

John: Not for the people who live there!

Meet the four currencies that are most widely traded (in order of popularity)

United States Dollar—*THE POWERHOUSE*

After World War II, nations met to choose one currency for all international trading. Because the United States held three-fourths of the world's gold at that time, the group picked the mighty US dollar.

European Euro—*THE NEWBIE*

In 2002, a dozen countries began using one currency called the euro (*YER-oh*) to make it easier to travel and trade. Today the euro is used in Austria, Belgium, Croatia, Cyprus, Estonia, Finland, France, Germany, Greece, Ireland, Italy, Lithuania, Luxembourg, Malta, the Netherlands, Portugal, Slovakia, Slovenia, and Spain. And did we mention Latvia?

Japanese Yen—*THE ASIAN SENSATION*

Japan has the sixth-largest population in Asia, but its currency—the yen (rhymes with *hen*)—is the most popular in the region.

British Pound—*THE OLD-TIMER*

In the fifteenth century, the British created a system for measuring gold and silver called the "troy weight system." At one point, a British pound coin weighed one troy pound. Not anymore. Today, the British pound is made of paper or plastic.

World Currency Symbols
(in alphabetical order by country)

The yuan (*yoo-AAN*) is the official currency of China.

The euro symbol comes from the Greek letter epsilon (**€**) and refers to the first letter of "Europe." The parallel lines in the middle are meant to show stability.

Guatemalan money is named after its national bird, the quetzal (*ket-SAAL*). This might be confusing if you're trying to buy a bird and have to ask, "How many quetzals is that quetzal?"

The symbol of the Indian rupee (*ROO-pee*) represents the country's history by combining the letter "ra" from the old Devanagari (*DAY-vuh-nah-guh-ree*) language and an English letter *R*. The stripes at the top are a nod to the national flag.

Yep, you've seen this before. The Japanese yen uses the same symbol as the Chinese yuan.

The złoty (*ZLAH-tee*) is the official currency of Poland and takes its name from the Polish word for "golden."

The State of Qatar (*KA-ter*) in the Persian Gulf calls its currency the Qatari riyal (*ree-YAHL*). Their bills come in lots of colors.

The United Kingdom's pound uses this symbol, which looks like a fancy letter *L*. It's mysterious because "pound" starts with the letter *p*. However, the word for pound in Latin is *libra*. Mystery solved!

The dollar sign appears in currencies across the globe, including the United States. The word "dollar" comes from coins minted in sixteenth-century Bohemia that were called "Joachimstaler" (*yo-AH-kim-stah-ler*). That was a long word for a small coin, so it got shortened to "taler," which sounds a lot like "dollar."

There's a theory that the US dollar sign evolved from the symbol for the Spanish peso (*PAY-soh*) along these lines:

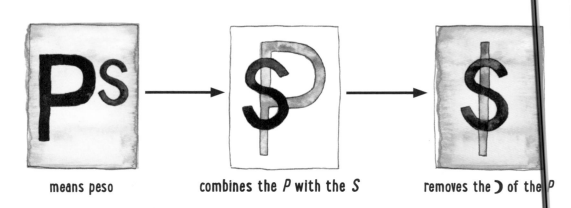

means peso   combines the *P* with the *S*   removes the) of the *P*

A cent—or penny—is one-hundredth of a dollar. Its sign comes from the first letter of the Latin word *centum*. Remember from the nickname "C-note" that centum means "one hundred"? (Want to guess how many years are in a century?)

PAPER MONEY

Mellody: John, come see. I'm creating my own design for money.

John: Why not use my face?

Mellody: Thanks, but no. My heart is set on an animal, but most of the ones I can draw have already been used on bills from around the world.

John: Sharks?

Mellody: Costa Rica did it.

John: Butterflies?

Mellody: On the Hong Kong dollar.

John: How about . . . a purple water buffalo?

Mellody: Check out the South African rand.

John: So what did you go with?

Mellody: A corgi!

FIVE INTERNATIONAL FACTS

1 The yuan (元) and renminbi (圓) are interchangeable terms for the same currency in the People's Republic of China. Renminbi means "people's money" in Mandarin.

2 If you shine a light through the maple leaf on a Canadian bill, the amount of money the note is worth will project onto a white background.

3 Rumor has it that Elizabeth II, the former queen of England, carried cash on Sundays so she could add money to the collection plate at church. Supposedly, a butler used to iron the ten-pound note into a tidy little square.

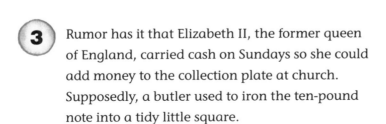

4 In the Middle Ages, people stored coins in small pots made from an orange clay material called "pygg." These "pygg pots" later evolved into actual pig shapes, so if you have a piggy bank, now you know why.

OINK!

5 In northern Italy, bankers used to do business on a bench—or *banca*—in the public square. If a banker didn't have money to pay his debts, the authorities would break his bench. A broken bench—or *banca rotta* (*BAHN-ka ROH-ta*)—became the English word "bankrupt."

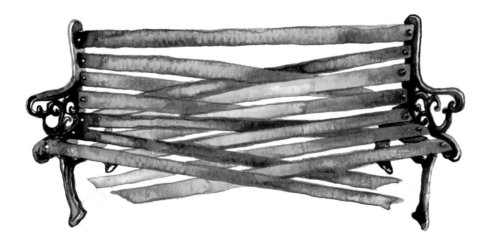

FUNNY PHRASES

There are many English phrases that people use
when talking about money, and some are very confusing.
Here are a cat and a bunny using some
common phrases along with their meanings.

Will work for treats!

Cat: Hey, Bunny. A penny for
        your thoughts?[1]
Bunny: Oh, I was just thinking
        about our friend Dog.

Cat: Why isn't he at the park?
Bunny: He's working. He got hired as a guide dog, which is good
        because he was really struggling to make ends meet.[2]

1 *A penny for your thoughts?*: What's on your mind?
2 *make ends meet*: earn enough money to pay for basic needs

Cat: So now he's on the clock.[3] Good gig?[4]

Bunny: Yeah. You know, I've been thinking about looking for a job.

Cat: Not me. I'm a cat. We're lazy.

Bunny: Well, I don't have two pennies to rub together,[5] and it's time I start saving for retirement when I'm old.

3 *on the clock*: working; employees often have to record the time when they arrive at and leave work

4 *gig*: a short-term job

5 *don't have two pennies to rub together*: poor

Cat: Anyhoo, I don't have to worry about money. My owner is loaded[6]—a real cash cow.[7]

Bunny: You're lucky that you were born with a silver spoon in your mouth.[8] Still, you know what they say: Money can't buy happiness.[9]

Cat: True. But it can buy a nice, stylish collar. Mine cost an arm and a leg.[10]

Bunny: Nice! Hey, now that Dog is making bank,[11] do you think he'll live high on the hog?[12]

6 *loaded*: rich, as in loaded down with bags of money

7 *cash cow*: something that generates lots of money or income

8 *born with a silver spoon in your mouth*: born into a family with wealth

9 *Money can't buy happiness*: money can buy things but not happy feelings

10 *cost an arm and a leg*: was really expensive

11 *making bank*: earning lots of money

12 *live high on the hog*: live well, as in be able to afford the best cuts of meat, which would be close to the belly or "high up" on the hog

Cat: Nah. He's always been a penny pincher.[13]

Bunny: And a penny saved is a penny earned.[14]

13 *penny pincher*: person who doesn't like to spend much money

14 *A penny saved is a penny earned*: if you make money and save it, rather than spend it, then you have truly earned it

Cat: When I have money, it just burns a hole in my pocket.[15] Which reminds me, Bunny, I'm still waiting for you to pay back that cash I loaned you.

Bunny: I can't. I'm flat broke. Busted. My wallet is empty. I'm strapped for cash. I am down and out.[16]

Cat: Really? Because someone dropped a dime[17] on you that you're holding some lettuce.[18]

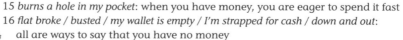

15 *burns a hole in my pocket*: when you have money, you are eager to spend it fast

16 *flat broke / busted / my wallet is empty / I'm strapped for cash / down and out*: all are ways to say that you have no money

17 *dropped the dime on*: told or informed on someone, referring to dropping a dime in an old pay phone to call the police

18 *lettuce*: cash

Bunny: Oh, I had some lettuce. But I ate it, and now I'm in the red.[19]
Cat: Deadbeat![20]
Bunny: My bad.

Cat: Oh, I can't stay mad at you. Tell you what, Bunny, that loan is on the house.[21]
Bunny: Really? Oh, Cat, you are worth your weight in gold.[22]

 19 *in the red*: in debt, a reference to the red ink used by accountants to record losses
20 *deadbeat*: someone who doesn't pay their debts
21 *on the house*: when something is given away for free
22 *worth your weight in gold*: having great value

MATH AND MONEY

Due to the price of metals, machinery, and labor, it costs a little more than two cents to make one US penny. Two cents to make one cent makes no sense!

There are 242 different combinations of pennies, nickels, dimes, and quarters that add up to one dollar. Here are some possible combinations:

Question: Would you rather have a million dollars *or* the amount you would get from a penny that doubles every day for thirty days?

Let's do the math on both choices:

First choice:

$1 million = $1 million

Second choice:

The sum of a penny doubled each day would be worth 64 cents after one week, $81.92 after two weeks, and $10,485.76 after three weeks. And by day thirty, that penny would be worth a whopping $5,368,709.12.

$		$		$	
Day 1	0.01	Day 11	10.24	Day 21	10,485.76
Day 2	0.02	Day 12	20.48	Day 22	20,971.52
Day 3	0.04	Day 13	40.96	Day 23	41,943.04
Day 4	0.08	Day 14	81.92	Day 24	83,886.08
Day 5	0.16	Day 15	163.84	Day 25	167,772.16
Day 6	0.32	Day 16	327.68	Day 26	335,544.32
Day 7	0.64	Day 17	655.36	Day 27	671,088.64
Day 8	1.28	Day 18	1310.72	Day 28	1,342,177.28
Day 9	2.56	Day 19	2621.44	Day 29	2,684,354.56
Day 10	5.12	Day 20	5242.88	Day 30	5,368,709.12

Answer: Choose the penny!

The doubling penny brainteaser shows how compound interest works. In short, money can earn money. If you put your money in an investment account that offers interest, your money will grow. And if you don't spend the growth, that growth will then grow. It's amazing!

Here's what to call a very large number if you see one:

Million = 1,000,000 **(six zeros)**

Billion = 1,000,000,000 **(nine zeros)**

Trillion = 1,000,000,000,000

(twelve zeros)

Googol* = 10,000,000,000,000,000,000,000,000,000,000,000,000,000,000,000,000,000,000,000,000,000,000,000,000,000,000,000,000,000,000,000,000,000 **(one hundred zeros)**

The company Google took its name from this large number but changed the spelling.

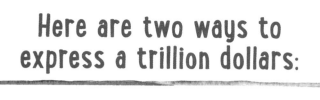

Here are two ways to express a trillion dollars:

A million million dollars = a trillion dollars (yep)

A thousand billion dollars = a trillion dollars (yep again)

Question: How many zeros are in a zillion?

Answer: It's a trick question! A zillion is not an actual number. It's a word that refers to an extremely large but unspecific amount.

PRICES THEN AND NOW (A.K.A. INFLATION)

The cost of goods—a fancy word for stuff—will go up and down over time for many reasons. Demand—how much people want something—plays a part. So does supply—how much of a product exists. Demand can be affected by fads or popularity. Supply can be affected by location or even weather. For example, during harvest months when there are more strawberries to buy, the price may be cheaper and more people may buy them. In colder months when there are fewer strawberries available, the price of strawberries goes up and fewer people may want them.

Because of many factors, prices tend to rise over time. This is called "inflation" (*in-FLAY-shen*). Due to inflation, someone today will have to spend more money to buy the same item that their grandparents bought over fifty years ago. Compare the prices on these seven items*:

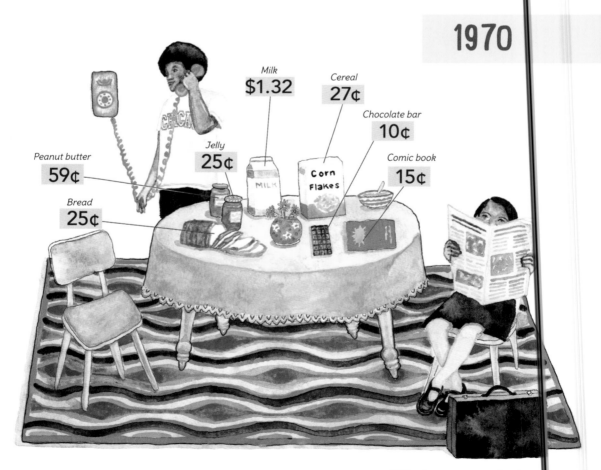

1970

Milk
$1.32

Cereal
27¢

Chocolate bar
10¢

Jelly
25¢

Comic book
15¢

Peanut butter
59¢

Bread
25¢

*All prices are approximate.

Before you start wishing you could go back in time and get thirteen chocolate bars for the price of one today, remember that pay for workers usually rises along with inflation.

And—good news!—improvements in technology mean that the price of TVs and computers has gone down over the past forty years. For example, in 1983, the first cell phone cost $4,000. Now a smartphone can be bought for under $200.

PRICES IN 1970*:	
Box of cereal	27¢
Gallon of milk	$1.32
Comic book	15¢
Loaf of bread	25¢
Peanut butter	59¢
Jelly	25¢
Chocolate bar	10¢
Total:	$2.93

PRICES IN 2020*:	
Box of cereal	$3.49
Gallon of milk	$4.80
Comic book	$4.99
Loaf of bread	$2.99
Peanut butter	$3.29
Jelly	$2.59
Chocolate bar	$1.39
Total:	$23.54

SERIOUSLY?

Money Stinks
US dollar bills are loaded with bacteria and fecal matter (you know, poop). Canada, Vietnam, Israel, and other countries have switched from paper to plastic-based bills that can be wiped clean.

We Can Do It

Boys Get All the Credit
Before 1974, women in the United States often couldn't get credit cards unless they had husbands who were willing to sign their applications. Congress had to pass a law making it illegal for companies to deny applicants because of race, color, religion, nationality, gender, or marital status.

Give George Washington a Makeover
If you fold a dollar bill the long way, you can make George Washington look like a mushroom.

Man   Mushroom

Bill's Retirement

A dollar bill gets passed around for about six and a half years before it is "retired." Worn-out bills are shredded and sometimes recycled into items like roof shingles and fireplace logs.

No Tears for Tears

If a bill is torn, as long as you have more than half of it, just take it to a bank and they'll swap it for a whole bill.

Bulls and Bears

Investors are divided into "bulls" (people who believe the stock market will rise) and "bears" (people who think it will fall). No one knows for sure where these terms come from. One thought is that bulls attack by thrusting their horns *up* while bears attack by swiping their claws *down*.

For the Love of . . .

The First Epistle to Timothy in the Bible is often misquoted as "Money is the root of all evil." The actual quote is "*For the love of* money is the root of all evil." Big difference!

Check Your Couch

Americans throw away or lose $62 million in change each year. Most of these coins are tossed in trash cans by mistake or disappear in sofas.

CHANGE IT UP

Mellody: I found all these coins in my sofa and put them in a jar. How much money do you think is in there?

John: Hmm. No idea.

Mellody: Me neither. Want to count them?

John: No. Just grab the jar and follow me.

Mellody: I didn't know there were machines that count coins.

John: Yep. You'll find them at most grocery stores.

Mellody: I like counting coins, but the machine is faster.

John: The total came to sixteen dollars and seven cents—three bills and three coins.

Mellody: I know it's the same amount of money, but now the jar looks kind of empty.

John: What should we do?

Mellody: Hey, let's check *your* couch!

GET TO KNOW BEN
(FRANKLIN, THAT IS)

Bills are great for buying stuff. They're also miniature works of art. Have you noticed that every US bill includes a portrait?

It makes sense that George Washington was the first president and is on the $1 bill. But that pattern doesn't continue. Abraham Lincoln was the sixteenth president, but there's no $16 bill. Lincoln is on the $5 bill. Remember, Alexander Hamilton wasn't a president at all, and he's on the $10 bill. Andrew Jackson, the seventh prez, is on the $20 bill, but in 2030 he will be replaced by Harriet Tubman, who escaped from slavery and helped free people via the Underground Railroad. She was also a spy for the Union army during the Civil War. Tubman will be the first Black person on a US bill.

Ben Franklin wasn't a president either, but his bill is the most popular. There are more $100 bills in circulation than $1 bills, so let's take a closer look.

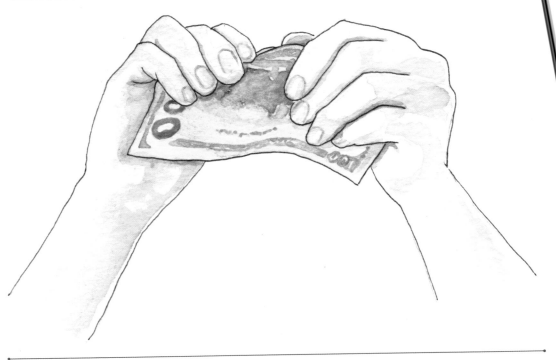

Bills are printed on a blend of two fabrics—linen and cotton—which makes them hard to rip. It takes four thousand double folds, forward and backward, to tear a dollar bill in two. (And, remember, if the bill *does* get torn, a bank will replace it.)

On Ben's Front

1

Check out Benjamin Franklin's portrait. What was he thinking? Maybe "Why didn't I put my hair in a man bun?"

The original 1914 C-note had a smaller picture of Ben on the front, while the back showed figures representing Labor, Plenty, America, Peace, and Commerce. In 1929, these figures were replaced by a drawing of Philadelphia's Independence Hall. Over the years, the design has been updated to stop counterfeiters (*kown-ter-FIT-ers*). Counterfeiters try to make fake money to buy real stuff, which is a crime.

FRANKLIN

2 High-tech ink contains metallic flakes that react to light. Color-changing ink appears in two places on the bill: on the big 100 in the lower-right corner and on the copper-colored inkwell, which has a green bell that appears and disappears when you tilt the bill. This special ink is sold only to the US government.

A quill, like the one used to sign the Declaration of Independence, appears to the right of Ben.

L12

3 Did you know a bill tells you where it was born? There are twelve regional Federal Reserve banks, and each location has its own letter and number combination: A1 = Boston; B2 = New York City; C3 = Philadelphia; D4 = Cleveland; E5 = Richmond, Virginia; F6 = Atlanta; G7 = Chicago; H8 = St. Louis; I9 = Minneapolis; J10 = Kansas City, Missouri; K11 = Dallas; and L12 = San Francisco.

Secretary of the Treasury.

Treasurer of the United States

4 Signatures from the secretary of the Treasury and the treasurer of the United States appear on the lower left. These signatures should be easy to read, so if you want either of these jobs, practice your penmanship.

100 100 100 100 10
100 100 100 100 100
100 100 100 100
100 100
100

Don't even try to reproduce a US banknote on a printer. Small yellow 100s trigger software that stops the copying process.

5 A blue 3D security ribbon is woven into the paper. When you tilt the note, the bells inside the strip turn into 100s.

6 The words "The United States of America" are hidden in Ben Franklin's jacket collar in teeny-tiny print. Can you read them?

7 Rub Ben Franklin's right shoulder on the bill with your finger. It's intentionally rough to the touch.

8 Some words from the opening of the Declaration of Independence appear to the right of Ben's portrait.

July 4, 1776.

9 The seal of the Treasury has a key and scales—not fish scales but the kind of scales you could weigh a fish on

10 A serial number is a unique combination of numbers and letters that appears twice on the front of the note. The first letter of the serial number tells you the year that the bill was printed (for example, J = 2009). The last letter cycles through the alphabet. The letters *O* and *Z* aren't used because *O* looks like a zero and *Z* is reserved for test prints.

ML 00532160 B

 If you hold the bill up to a light while looking at the building, you can see Ben's ghost on the left-hand side. Spooky, huh?

On Ben's Back

1

US banknotes used to display the phrase *E pluribus unum*, which is Latin for "Out of many, one." That phrase referred to the states that united to form one country. In 1956, Congress voted to swap in the current phrase,

IN GOD WE TRUST

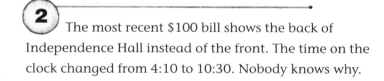

2 The most recent $100 bill shows the back of Independence Hall instead of the front. The time on the clock changed from 4:10 to 10:30. Nobody knows why.

3 More yellow 100s are on the backside.

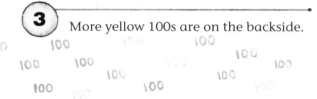

4 The HUGE 100 makes it easier for people who are visually impaired to not mistake a $100 bill for a $1 bill.

LET'S PLAY BANK

Mellody: Good morning, sir. Welcome to our bank branch. I'm your teller, and I'm here to serve the bank's customers. Will you be making a deposit—that means putting money in— or a withdrawal—that means taking money out?

John: I am making a deposit. I found these on the beach. It's pirate booty.

Mellody: Booty. Still cracks me up!

John: Okay, just pretend it's cash. You'll keep my deposit safe?

Mellody: Yes, that's what banks do. We keep track of your money, too.

John: Great. And how do I turn my deposit back into cash?

Mellody: You make a withdrawal in person, or you can use this plastic card connected to your account at an ATM machine. Do you know what ATM stands for?

John: Yes. *Activate the Money!*

Mellody: No.

John: *Abracadabra, There's Money!*

Mellody: No.

John: I give up.

Mellody: It stands for *Automated Teller Machine.*

John: Hmm. I like *Alien Treasure Maker* better.

Mellody: Me too! BTW—that means "by the way"—here are other ways to move money out of your bank account.

John: Let's hear them.

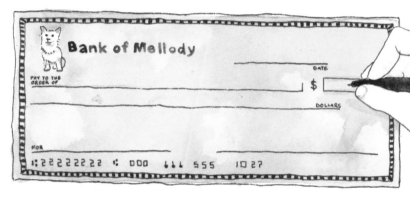

Mellody: You can write a check, tap your debit card, or use an app on your phone.

John: But those only work if I have money in the bank?

Mellody: Correct.

John: What if I don't have enough money to pay for something really big, like a car?

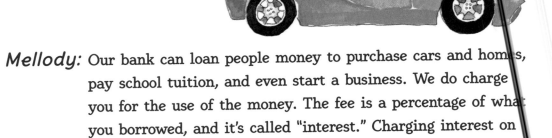

Mellody: Our bank can loan people money to purchase cars and homes, pay school tuition, and even start a business. We do charge you for the use of the money. The fee is a percentage of what you borrowed, and it's called "interest." Charging interest on loans is one way that a bank makes money.

John: Hey, I'd like to start a business. Can I please have a loan?

Mellody: You'll have to speak to our loan officer. One moment, please.

Mellody: Hello. I'm the loan officer. Would you like a business loan?

John: Yes.

Mellody: Are you eighteen years old?

John: Not yet.

Mellody: Then legally you're too young. Sorry. I'll go get the teller.

Mellody: Hello. How'd it go?

John: Not great. I didn't really care for that loan officer.

Mellody: She doesn't make the rules. Any other questions?

John: Yeah, what's that door over there?

Mellody: That's our vault. If you'd like a tour,
I can get the security guard.

John: Yes, please.

Mellody: Hello. I'm the security guard. Please follow me.

John: Wow. That door is very thick.

Mellody: It weighs four tons. That's eight thousand pounds.

John: Wow. There are so many drawers!

Mellody: These are safe-deposit boxes. Some people keep their valuable items here.

John: To protect them from theft?

Mellody: And natural disasters like fires, floods, and hurricanes.

John: What are some things people put in safe-deposit boxes?

Mellody: Important papers like a birth certificate or a passport. The boxes could also contain jewelry or military medals . . . or a special piece of yarn.

John: You really love that yarn. Where's it from?

Mellody: Can't tell you. Tour's over!

Mellody: Welcome back, sir. Did you enjoy your tour?

John: Yes, although it ended a little abruptly.

Mellody: Hey, did I tell you about the bank's foreign money exchange?

John: Not yet. But I bet you will now.

Mellody: Before you travel, you can bring American dollars to the bank and we'll give you the same amount in another country's currency . . . minus a small fee. Do you need any euros today?

John: Not today.

Mellody: Well, if you change your mind, we're here. In fact, there are more than seventy-five thousand bank branch offices in the United States. If you pass one, stop in and say hi!

John: I will.

Mellody: And here's a pen to show our appreciation.

John: Thank you! Although I don't really need a pen. Hey, can I trade this pen for a cupcake?

FINAL FACTS TO FILE AWAY

Quarters and dimes used to be made with pure metals, so minters added ridges to make it obvious if someone tried to file down the edges and collect the shavings. Although coins are no longer made of pure metal, the ridges remain and help people who are blind or vision impaired tell the difference between a quarter and a nickel or a dime and a penny.

A commodity (*kuh-MAH-duh-tee*) is a raw material that is sold in a large quantity and then later processed into smaller products. For example, a crop of corn is a commodity that can be sold to different factories and turned into cereal, popcorn, corn syrup, cornstarch, wax paper, and other things.

There are two basic kinds of commodities. Soft commodities are grown. They include corn, wheat, rice, and soybeans. Hard commodities are dug up from deep underground. They include oil, helium, and precious metals like gold, platinum, and silver. Do you know how those metals got into the earth in the first place? (Hint: I told you all about meteorites at the beginning of the book.)

Why do people throw coins in fountains? Because it's considered good luck to offer a gift while making a wish. At the Trevi Fountain in Rome, the legend says that if a person tosses a coin over their shoulder into the fountain, they will return to Rome. (Good for the tourism business!) Each week visitors supposedly toss more than $24,000 worth of coins into the Trevi Fountain. That adds up to $1,248,000 a year, which gets donated to charity.

PRICELESS

Mellody: The book is almost done. I had fun so I'm sad it's over.

John: Don't be sad! Do you have a favorite fact?

Mellody: Not exactly a favorite, but now that I know most dollar bills have little bits of poop on them, I'm going to wash my hands after turning George Washington into a mushroom.

John: I told my mom that all metals on earth came from space. She didn't even know that and she's an adult.

Mellody: Lots of people don't know that much about money, which is weird because everyone needs it to live.

John: I still have a lot of questions about money. And I have one other question that only you can answer.

Mellody: What is it?

John: I know it's personal, but since we're friends, can you tell me why you think that piece of yarn is so special?

Mellody: Okay, but you have to pinkie promise not to make fun of me.

John: Pinkie me.

Mellody: See, when I was a baby, my grandma crocheted me an orange blanket. I loved that blanket and brought it everywhere. Eventually, it wore out. Now this is all that's left. I know to you, it just looks like a piece of yarn. But to me, it's priceless.

John: Priceless? You mean, it's not worth anything?

Mellody: Just the opposite. Priceless means it's *so* valuable that you can't put a price on it.

John: Ah. I get it. Some things are worth more than money.

Mellody: Exactly! I keep the yarn in my wallet, so in a way, my blanket is still with me. And so is my grandmother.

John: That's really nice. Thanks for telling me.

Mellody: I'm glad you know.

John: Hey, I just had an idea. Maybe one day we could work together.

Mellody: That sounds fun. Who will be in charge?

John: Both of us. We can co-lead. You in?

Mellody: I'm in!

John: Let's do this!

Mellody: Yeah! But maybe we should learn long division first.

Index